COASTERS IN COLOUR

Bernard McCall and Ian Willett

Copyright © Bernard McCall and Ian Willett 1996

First published in the United Kingdom by Bernard McCall
400 Nore Road, Portishead, Bristol, BS20 8EZ

ISBN 0 9513576 6 2

Printed by D. Brown and Sons Ltd, Bridgend

INTRODUCTION

The sheer variety of coastal cargo vessels which trade in the waters around western Europe makes for two problems in compiling a photographic survey. Firstly there is the difficulty of what to include and what to leave out. This leads to the second problem, namely that of deciding how to present and classify such diverse material. The solution to the first problem must inevitably remain the personal choice of the authors. They must hope that their choices will also engage the interest of the reader. As to how to present the material, the decision on this occasion has been to follow the time-honoured format of the A to Z listing. This has the virtue of being easy to follow and logical in its approach. The letters of the alphabet have been used in a flexible way so as to emphasise that basic diversity in the subject matter.

Diversity, then, is the first theme which emerges. Diversity in the design, age, nationality and ownership of the vessels themselves is complemented by the diversity of the cargoes they carry and the harbours they visit. Key letters are used to indicate any or all of these characteristics. There are pitfalls of course. The letter "x", for instance, has led to some nifty lateral thinking, the effectiveness of which only the reader can judge. Coasters called the *Xanthence* or *Xandrina* have eluded the viewfinders arrayed here. A second theme will become apparent in these photographs. This relates to the role of coastal shipping in the general transport scene. Each of the major transport modes has a role to which it is better suited than the others. There remains a suspicion in some minds that coastal shipping, like the railways, never quite achieves the proverbial "level playing field" in our national transport planning.

Bernard McCall (Portishead)
Ian Willett (Epping)
January 1996

ACKNOWLEDGEMENTS

The authors wish to place on record their debt to many who have provided assistance with this book. It is often difficult to pick out individuals but special thanks must go to Cedric Catt and Richard Potter for their specialised knowledge; to Roger Scott and Simon Leafe, of Leafe & Hawkes Ltd (Hull), W. N. Lindsay (Stevedores) Ltd. (Berwick) and Alasdair Moodie, of Osprey Shipping (Avonmouth), for specific help in obtaining some photographs; to the following publications : *Lloyd's Register of Shipping, Modern River Sea Traders* (by Chris Cheetham), *Everard of Greenhithe* (by K. S. Garrett), the magazines *Ships Monthly, Sea Breezes, Coastal Shipping* and *Marine News* (the journal of the World Ship Society); and to Gil Mayes, who checked the text and eliminated errors. We also offer our thanks to Roy Morris and the staff of D Brown and Sons Ltd, our printers.

Front cover : *Union Transport's* Union Jupiter *was built at the now-closed yard of Cochrane Shipbuilders, Selby, and launched on 16 November 1989 and was officially named at a ceremony alongside* HMS Belfast *on 6 April 1990. With a length of a fraction under 100 metres, she was the forerunner of a class designed to be the longest possible capable of navigation up the River Ouse to Goole, thus giving the nickname "Goolemax" to the design. She is a frequent caller at ports in southern England and we see her leaving Teignmouth on 13 April 1995.* BM

Back cover : *The* Jubilence *was photographed at Tweed Dock, Berwick, on 21 September 1990. She was built at the shipyard of J W Cook, also now sadly closed, at Wivenhoe on the north side of the River Colne downriver from Colchester. Along with sistership* Insistence, *she was a useful member of the fleet of Crescent Shipping and was usually to be seen trading between ports in eastern England and the near Continent. In mid-1994, she was sold to Caribbean owners and made her way across the Atlantic to the West Indies. A year later, it was reported that she had been renamed* Dolly *and was flying the flag of Belize.* IW

As we are making our way through the alphabet, it is appropriate that we begin with the *Alpha;* alpha being the first letter of the Greek alphabet. The ship has a had a long life for she is still trading at the time of writing, having been built almost forty years earlier. She was built in 1956 at the **A**dler Werft shipyard in Bremen and her original name was *Star.* In 1968 she was renamed *Alpha* and kept this name for 20 years before being renamed *Ralph.* If this was a somewhat unimaginative name change, it took an equal lack of imagination to change her name back to *Alpha* for a short time in 1989 before she was renamed *Don,* again in 1989. In 1991, she was sold at auction to Capt. Mike Clayton who traded her as *Don* under the St Vincent and Grenadines flag into the following year. In 1992 she became the *Rema* under the Honduran flag and was operated by Halcyon Shipping, of Great Yarmouth, although ownership was credited to Herbert Shipping Ltd., of Plymouth. In the late summer of 1995, she was sold to Turkish Cypriot owners and on 18 September she left Teignmouth with a cargo of clay for Piraeus as part of her delivery voyage to the Mediterranean, to be renamed *Suna 2* in early October. We see her here on 9 March 1980 at Purton as she navigates the canal linking Sharpness to Gloucester with a cargo of pig iron for the latter port. This waterway is sadly underused by commercial shipping.

(Cedric Catt)

The River Avon is now little used by commercial shipping, seeing only one or two coasters which call each year to load heavy lift cargoes such as silos (see page 13). The last cargo-carrying ships to use the City Docks on a regular basis were sand dredgers which discharged at Hotwells. In the last few months of trade, the *Arco Scheldt* was a regular caller and was photographed in the Avon Gorge on 16 June 1990. One of the largest vessels of her type to sail up the Avon, she was built by **A**ppledore Shipbuilders in 1972 and was initially named *Amey III*, a name which lasted less than a year because Amey Marine Ltd became ARC Marine.

Bell Lines has developed into one of the leading transportation companies in Europe. Its sea transport division services terminals in the Netherlands (Rozenburg), France (Radicatel), the UK (Teesport, Avonmouth, Ipswich, Greenock) and Ireland (Waterford, Belfast). Between 1976 and 1978, a series of nine container ships was delivered by the Japanese Kagoshima Dock and Iron Works Company to various owners for charter to Bell Lines. The *Bell Racer* was a 1977 delivery and, along with the *Bell Ruler*, she was lengthened in 1984. In December 1993, Bell Lines left their own Bellport terminal on the River Usk at Newport and transferred their south west UK terminal to Avonmouth. Soon after the move, the *Bell Racer* was photographed passing **B**attery Point, Portishead, on 24 December 1993 following her departure from Avonmouth for Waterford. Battery Point is an ideal location for shipwatching though it has also played its part in the history of the area. In Elizabethan times, it served as a watch tower and it was held as a fort by the Royalists during the Civil War.

BM 5

The port of **B**erwick at the mouth of the River Tweed has enjoyed a significant revival in the mid-1990s, thanks to the widening of the dock entrance. Mostly bulk commodities are handled, including cement, fertilisers and barley. It is the latter cargo for delivery to **B**remen which is being loaded on to the *Breydon*

Venture on 1 April 1993. She was built in 1977 by the Yorkshire Drydock Co Ltd, in Hull. Originally named *Wis*, she took her current name of *Breydon Venture* in 1986. In late 1995, it was announced that she had been sold for conversion to a bunkering tanker for work on the River Humber.   *IW*

The late evening sun catches the *BP Springer* at the Shetland island of **B**ressay on 25 July 1993. This coastal tanker was built by Hall Russell, Aberdeen, and launched as the *Dublin* on 4 December 1968. Further details of one of her near sisters will be found on page 32. The *Dublin* became *BP Springer* in 1976. From the mid-1980s, she was dedicated to the distribution of oil products from BP's Grangemouth refinery to ports and jetties in the Scottish highlands and islands, often visiting between three and six different locations on any single voyage. Her calls at Bressay occur at approximately 3-monthly intervals and on this voyage she also visited Kirkwall (Orkney), Stornoway (Lewis) and Portree (Skye).

BM

7

C is for commodities and we begin with China clay. Resisting the temptation to look at the much-photographed port of Charlestown on the outskirts of St. Austell, we focus on Par some 7 km east of Charlestown. Although it lacks the charm of Charlestown and the grandeur of nearby Fowey, the clay dries in the background make this port instantly recognisable. The focus of our attention on 11 April 1995 is the *Lady Elsie*. Built by the Bodewes Gruno yard at Foxhol in 1975, she entered the fleet of Beck's at Groningen as *Velox*, serving this company for

thirteen years. In 1988, she was purchased by Harris & Dixon and was renamed *Canvey*. After a further four years, she entered the fleet of the Rochester-based Thomas Watson (Shipping) Ltd, nominally owned by Andrean Shipping Ltd. Watson vessels have traditionally been named "*Lady* _____ " and the *Canvey* became *Lady Elsie*. She has spent much time on charter to Cardiff-based Charles Willie & Co (Shipping) Ltd, working on routes between the UK and the Iberian peninsula.

The port of Goole owes its very existence to the Yorkshire coalfield whose output used to be exported from the port in vast tonnages. The decline in the demand for coal and the gradual exhaustion of the traditional coalfields linked to Goole by a network of canals have seen the port search out and win a wide variety of new cargoes. The port's infrastructure has had to be adapted to these new cargoes and this has resulted in the demolition of many items of industrial archaeological interest. A case in point is the coal hoist seen here on 20 November 1977.

The coaster is the *Mariane V*. She was a 1955 product of the Stader shipyard, in Stade, and was built as the *Atlantis*. To increase her earning potential, she was lengthened in 1968. She became *Mariane V* in 1974 and kept this name for ten years before being renamed *Vespa 1* in 1984 after purchase by Cypriot owners although she remained a regular caller at east coast U K ports. Her working career ended when she arrived at Rotterdam from Perth on 5 March 1986. She was sold for demolition in Belgium in the autumn of 1987.

BM

The ever-changing demands of customers and the good or bad harvests which result from the vagaries of climate ensure that cereals are being transported, often by sea, throughout the year. The transshipment trades have regularly provided steady employment for coasters and ports such as Selby receive cargoes brought from larger ports such as Rotterdam. The *Guy Chipperfield* was photographed at Selby on 24 August 1980. She was built in 1974 at the Bodewes Bergum yard, now one of the Damen group shipyards. In 1982, she was renamed *Ellen W* after purchase by W B Woolley Scotland Ltd, her current owners now being Tara Shipping Ltd. She continues to call regularly at Selby.

BM

Photography of ships in **d**rydock is not easy. Problems such as excessive shade and sheer size of vessel when in a small drydock combined with sometimes awkward angles can all pose problems. Thankfully, none of these was evident when the *Ernest 1* was photographed in the Bute Drydock, Cardiff, on 15 August 1989. This coaster was built at Clelands, Wallsend, in 1967 for F T Everard and Sons, for whom she traded as the *Apricity* until 1982. She was one of a pair, the other being the *Actuality,* and it was the owner's aim to operate them in the timber trade from Scandinavia to Gunness on the River Trent. To maximise their deadweight capacity, their construction was kept as light as possible. However, rapid improvements in ship design soon made them obsolete in the trade for which they had been built and in 1974 they were refitted to enable them to trade more generally. The Newbury engine was replaced by a lighter Mirrlees Blackstone engine and their derricks and winches were removed. In late 1982, the *Apricity* was sold to Carisbrooke Shipping and renamed *Heleen C*, the *Actuality* following her into Carisbrooke ownership as the *Greta C* a few months later after

spending a short time as the *Hughina* in the ownership of Allsworth Shipping. Our subject worked for Carisbrooke for six years before being sold in late 1988 and renamed *Ernest T* at the beginning of 1989. It was while she was in drydock that ownership changed yet again and it took a few swift brush strokes to rename her *Ernest 1*. Her owners were reported to be Denver Shipping Ltd, of Bandar Abbas, Iran. After leaving drydock, she loaded metal shavings at Cardiff and departed on 9 September for Bilbao. She made little progress for she sent out a distress signal when in the Western Approaches and had to be towed back to Falmouth with engine trouble. It was not until 13 January 1990 that she departed from Falmouth - but she was forced to put back later that day for further repairs. It was reported at the time that her new owners intended to reinstate her cargo gear for work in the Middle East. In 1991, she was renamed *Shad 1*. Current information suggests that she has one derrick, so at least some cargo gear may have been replaced.

BM

Denmark has a wealth of interest for shiplovers. Its many islands are serviced by a wide variety of ferries but they also generate a considerable amount of dry cargo traffic. Thankfully much of this traffic is transported by water so driving on Danish roads is a much more enjoyable experience than on British roads. Apart from the free port area of Copenhagen and a couple of private ports, the dock areas are open and welcoming so quaysides tend to be frequented by casual and enthusiast visitors especially in the evenings. The port of Marstal on the island of Aero will be familiar to many as a port of registry on many Danish coasters.

It is also renowned for building and repairing vessels. This photograph, taken at Marstal on 31 July 1993, well illustrates the extensive influence of this port. The blue-hulled *Hanne Hansen* has kept her name since being built in 1958 at the H C Christensen shipyard, in Marstal. She is registered in the port, as is the red-hulled *Lindholm*. She is a 1952-built product of the Hugo Peters yard, at Wewelsfleth, and was named *Ingrid* until 1959. Both coasters have been lengthened, the *Lindholm* in 1964 and the *Hanne Hansen* in 1966.

BM

Deck cargoes can be a navigator's nightmare! Not only do they have to be stowed and lashed with the utmost care but they can have a marked effect on the navigation task with problems of stability, wind resistance and visibility. The skipper of the *RMS Westfalia* will be pleased that his ship is making a short voyage across the Bristol Channel from Bristol to Barry with two silos on 18 August 1994. Such cargoes still bring ships up the River Avon to lock into the City Docks, for the builders of the silos have a factory near to the Cumberland Basin so road transport is kept to a minimum. The *RMS Westfalia* was built in 1980 by C Luehring at Brake as the *Atoll*. She kept this name until early 1992 when she was renamed *Karin E* and a little over a year later, she became *RMS Westfalia*.

The River Elbe sees a wide variety of vessels. The majority are bound to and from Hamburg or a handful of smaller ports along the Elbe while others in the lower reaches of this mighty river are heading to or from the Kiel Canal whose western end joins the Elbe at Brunsbuttel. The *Ria* is typical of the small coasters which are to be seen on the Elbe, many handling cargo transshipped from ocean-going vessels in Hamburg. She was built in 1960 at the small yard of Gebr. Schuerenstedt at Bardenfleth on the River Weser. Her original name was *Moni*. She relinquished this in favour of *Castor* in 1965, then becoming *Thea K* in 1970 and finally *Ria* in 1989. Always kept in immaculate condition, such vessels are a delight to behold, especially with their wooden wheelhouses. Here we see her heading up the Elbe, seemingly in ballast, on 1 June 1989.

IW

The name of F T Everard and Sons Ltd has been at the forefront of shipowning in the United Kingdom throughout this century and has always operated a fleet that could be easily adapted to the ever-changing demands of coastal shipping. Chosen as illustrative is the *Singularity,* one of a class of four vessels built in the late 1970s. She was built by Swan Hunter Shipbuilders Ltd at the Readhead Shipyard in South Shields and had the dubious distinction of being the final ship built at this yard. It had been intended that she would represent the British coastal fleet at the 1977 Spithead Jubilee Review but industrial action during her construction meant that the timing of her completion was uncertain and her place at the Review was taken by the *Fred Everard*. This was unfortunate as Everard's previous *Singularity* had been present at the 1953 Spithead Review. Of the four ships in her class, the new *Singularity* and her sistership *Jack*

Wharton were the only two built with cargo-handling gear. Both were intended for more than coastal work, and the *Singularity* made two voyages to Brazil in 1979, sailing 1,000 miles up the River Amazon to Manaos. Two years later, she passed through the Panama Canal on passage to Colombia. After the Falklands conflict, she made several voyages to Ascension and Port Stanley with military stores and equipment. However, the two gearless ships in the class proved to be more adaptable and so the *Singularity* (and *Jack Wharton*) were sold in 1987. With minimal effort, she was renamed *Singolarita* by her new Italian owners and, now registered in Naples, she continues to trade successfully for them, usually in the Mediterranean. Here we view her from Penarth Head on 9 June 1983 as she leaves Cardiff with a cargo of steel for Wahran.

BM

The transport and disposal of effluent has become an environmentally sensitive issue in recent years. During the 1970s, Effluents Services Ltd. built up a small fleet of tankers dedicated to the disposal of effluents at sea but this fleet has now diminished in the wake of ever stricter legislation about such disposal. The *Anglezarke* was acquired by the company in 1975. She had been built in 1956 as the *Nessand* by the Schlichtingwerft yard at Travemunde. In 1967, she became the *Otto* and then *Otto Terkol* in the following year. After only three years in the Terkildsen & Olsen fleet, she was sold and renamed *Mabuli*. It was in 1975 that she was bought by Effluents Services Ltd, and in common with other vessels owned by this company she was named after a reservoir in the north of England. She was eventually demolished at Garston in July 1988. During her 13 years in ESL colours, she was often to be seen working out of Goole and this photograph shows her outward bound in the River Ouse on 22 July 1980.

BM

Despite claims to the contrary, there is little evidence that alternatives to road transport are actively sought in the UK. The last twenty years have seen a considerable increase in road transport, the consequences of which are all too apparent to those who have to use the UK's increasingly congested roads. In 1985, the Esso depot on the River Ely in Cardiff closed, following a decision to concentrate the import of oil products to Avonmouth with onward distribution by road - thus adding further to the congestion on the Severn Bridge. One of the final deliveries to the Ely terminal was brought from Fawley on 7 July 1985 by a regular caller, the *Otto*. This tanker has kept her original name since her launch at the Krogerwerft Yard in Rendsburg in 1970, and she was lengthened in 1976. The enormous tidal range in the Bristol Channel is graphically illustrated by this low water view - the river is little more than a trickle. The approach to the jetty from Cardiff Roads was tricky and the *Otto*, without the benefit of a bow thruster, would have required tug assistance to berth and unberth. This would add to the operational expenses.

The Firth of Forth sees a wide variety of shipping, much of it generated by the BP oil refinery at Grangemouth. The Forth road bridge is a popular vantage point for watching the passing shipping and it is from here that the *Danish Dart* was observed heading for Grangemouth. She is the second of a pair of tankers built in 1976 for BP Danmark A/S at the Svendborg Shipyard, the first one being named *Danish Arrow*. Both are liquefied gas tankers which are capable of carrying various gases such as propane or butane in their four horizontal tanks. Built with an Ice Class 3 certificate, both ships are ideally suited to trading in Scandinavia and visits to Grangemouth have become increasingly rare since this photograph was taken on 18 April 1981. She sailed to Esbjerg two days later.

BM

Containerisation (an ugly word!) has made a massive impact on virtually all modes of transport. As far as ships are concerned, it has spawned a breed of vessel growing ever-larger each year. These large container ships function most economically when calling at a limited range of ports in set sequence and to a fixed timetable. Seaborne delivery and distribution of containers is undertaken by feeder ships which maintain links with the ports used by larger ships. A good example of such a feeder is the *Freesia*, built in 1983 at the Wewelsfleth yard of Hugo Peters for Stade-based owner Heinz Freese. She has spent her life working under the "Unifeeder" banner linking Hamburg and Bremerhaven to Copenhagen, Aarhus, Helsingborg and Gothenburg. Here we see her heading west in the Kiel Canal on 1 August 1991.

BM

G is for the small Lancashire port of **G**lasson Dock at the mouth of the Lune estuary and some 8 kilometres from Lancaster to which city it is joined by the Lancaster Canal. This busy port now handles varied cargoes including imports of grain and sand. It also fulfils an important role serving the Isle of Man with bulk cargoes and building materials. Much of this trade is handled by ships in the Ramsey-based fleet of Mezeron Ltd. **G** is also for *Greeba River,* the largest of the three vessels in the Mezeron fleet at the time of writing. This vessel was built at Martenshoek in 1969 for the well-known Dutch coaster owners, Beck's of Groningen. Originally named *Apollo 1*, she moved to Arklow Shipping in 1980 and was renamed *Arklow River.* Two years later, she became the *Cynthia June*, and then *Tora* in 1986. After being renamed *Greeba River* in 1988, she has been a regular trader across the Irish Sea.

BM

On 11 May 1975, not only is the *Gladonia* at her home port but also at her birthplace, too - the port of **G**oole. She was built by the now-defunct Goole shipyard in 1963 for J Wharton (Shipping) Ltd, a familiar British owner of coastal vessels. Sold by this company in the Spring of 1985, she arrived at Barry on 26 March 1985 to load second-hand vehicles and spares for delivery to the West Indies. It was intended that she herself would be sold in that area. She left Barry on 17 April for Georgetown (Guyana). The intended plans did not come to fruition and some months later she came back across the Atlantic to Portugal. By the end of 1985, she had been named *Integrity* under the Honduran flag. On 21 January 1986, she left Rouen with a cargo of grain which, strange to say, she brought to Barry. There then followed a period of lay-up before she was sold to Avonmouth-based Runwave Ltd who sought and obtained permission for her to be renamed *Gladonia*. She returned to the British flag and for a few days, she was registered in Goole before this was changed to Gibraltar. She left Barry on 15 February 1987 and crossed the Bristol Channel to sail up the River Avon for drydocking in the former Albion Drydock of Charles Hill's Bristol shipyard. She remained in the Runwave fleet until September 1994 when she was sold to Egyptian owners but without change of name. In mid-November, she arrived at Setubal but legal problems arose over her damaged cargo of rice and she was arrested. She later secretly slipped away from the port and was last reported at Bizerta undergoing repairs in late November, 1995. One wonders what other dramas she faces in what has been a chequered career.

BM

Green is certainly an unusual colour for a ship to be painted and *Gore* is just as unusual as a name. The vessel was built at Selby in 1969 as the *Eloquence*, and she traded under this name for Crescent Shipping until 1985. She was then purchased by Brian Cuckow, of Rainham, Kent, and was renamed - and repainted.

We see her at Otterham Quay on 2 August 1986. Her new identity lasted only two years for she moved to Dennison Shipping Ltd in 1987 and was renamed *Holm Sound*. This takes us conveniently to our next letter, H.

BM

Indeed, our first **H** is the *Holm Sound* herself. The family-owned Dennison Shipping Ltd, of Kirkwall, grew from modest beginnings to a 6-ship fleet in the early 1990s. In 1994, however, it was troubled by financial problems and was forced to cease its shipowning activities and go into receivership. The only Dennison-owned vessel in the fleet at the time (the others were chartered) and the last to be sold was the *Holm Sound* - all of the coasters were named after Sounds in Orkney or Shetland. After a period laid up at Burray, Orkney, she reverted to ownership in Rainham when she was bought by Gardscreen Shipping Ltd. She had the misfortune to suffer a major engine failure on her delivery voyage and had to be towed to Stromness. Eventually she was re-engined and returned to commercial operation during Spring 1995, delivering stone from the Isle of Grain to ports in Kent and in the ownership of Radmoor Shipping Ltd. Our photograph sees the *Holm Sound* in Dennison ownership and arriving at Berwick to load cement on 17 July 1990.

We stay at Berwick and we stay with a Scottish shipowner for Hay & Company provides us with our second letter **H**. This company, founded in 1844 by William Hay and two of his sons, eventually grew to become one of the best known Shetland firms. As general merchants, they owned shops in several Shetland communities and were the islands' largest importers of coal and timber. They also played a vital role in the development of the Shetland fishing industry, both as fishcurers and as owners of fishing vessels. In February 1954, Hay & Company returned to shipowning after a gap of 40 years when it purchased the steamer *Thorn*. This vessel was renamed *Columbine* after the company's last sailing vessel which had been withdrawn from service in 1914. It became the company policy to give the name *Shetland*

Trader to the largest vessel in the fleet and the current holder of this name was purchased in March 1979. She was built in 1972 at the shipyard of J Bolson in Poole. Originally named *Parkesgate*, she entered service in the ownership of Hull Gates Shipping, thus providing a second link with the letter **H**. From 1974, she spent much time on charter delivering steel from the giant Hoogovens steelworks at Ijmuiden to U K ports such as Whitby, Rochester, Poole and King's Lynn. From 1979 onwards, she has given valiant service to Hay & Company. One of her regular cargoes is the delivery of talc from Baltasound, Shetland, to Sharpness. She is also a frequent caller in ports on the east coast of England and Scotland.

IW

A high vantage point for ship photography is often welcomed for it gives a pleasing view of the vessel. There are professional companies which specialise in aerial photography; the amateur has to rely on suitable bridges. In the U K, the Severn, Forth and Humber bridges all offer suitable viewpoints but it is the latter bridge which will appeal most to coaster enthusiasts. Those readers who may be considering bridge photography for the first time are advised to choose a warm, sunny day - bridges can be windy, cold and desolate. Shelter and sustenance are often a long way off! What could be more appropriate here than observing the *Humber I* passing beneath the **Humber Bridge** on 7 August 1983. She is a 1966 product of the Krogerwerft yard in Rendsburg

and for the first nine years of her life, she traded as the *Germania*. In 1975, she became *Altair V* and then *Humber I* in 1979. Five years later, she was renamed *Rio Minho* and almost immediately *Humber*, retaining this latter name for a further four years. In the Spring of 1988, she left European waters, sailing from La Corunna on 3 May for Tampa and New York. By the summer of that year, she was trading in the U S Gulf. There then followed two more name changes in quick succession for she became *Cay Verde* in 1988 and *Melray* in 1989. In January 1992, she arrived at Savannah from Miami and we then seem to lose track of her.

BM

The *Inisheer* began life in 1985, a product of the Tille Shipyard at Kootstetille in the Netherlands. She was launched for German owners as *Elisa von Barssel* but soon changed her name to *Flagship I* and by early 1986 she was trading in the U S Gulf and West Indies, calling at ports such as Mobile, New Orleans, Houston and Port of Spain. At the end of the year, her operator was a Miami-based company and she was renamed *Lia Ventura*, changing the German flag for that of Cyprus, though her work kept her in the U S Gulf. By late 1987, she had returned to the German ownership of Gerhard Wessels, based in Haren, but before the end of the year she was bought by James Tyrrell, of Arklow, for operation within the Arklow Shipping group. Following a two-week stay in New York, she left on 1 December 1987 and arrived at Rotterdam on Christmas Day. From mid-April 1989, she found

herself linking Ellesmere Port to Belfast or Warrenpoint and it was while she was working this route that she was photographed in the River Mersey, off Eastham, on 26 July 1989. Within a year, she was working a regular service between Workington and Drogheda. She then entered a pattern which saw wider trading although Irish Sea work remained prominent. The next important stage in her career came when she arrived in her home port of Arklow on 1 March 1995. There she changed her name to *Dunkerque Express* in readiness to launch a new container service linking that French port to Antwerp, Europoort, Rotterdam and Felixstowe. An ideal multi-purpose vessel able to carry containers or general cargo, she has served her various owners well during her first decade.

BM

The Isle of Man flag is seen increasingly on coasters and much larger vessels. One of the fleets to use it is that of Stephenson Clarke Ltd. This company acquired Wm. Robertson Shipowners Ltd in 1970, along with the latter's fleet of ten ships, but it was not until 1978 that the two fleets were fully integrated. Robertson ships had traditionally been named after precious and semi-precious stones, and the owning company was indeed styled Gem Line Ltd. Happily, Stephenson Clarke kept the names of the Robertson ships which they acquired. The *Gem* was built in 1969 by the Nieuwe Noord Nederlandse yard at Groningen. In 1990, she was sold to Syrian owners and renamed *Damask Rose* for trading in the Mediterranean. She became *Anis Rose* in September 1995. In this view, she is approaching Barry on 29 August 1985 to load a cargo of cement clinker for Magheramorne, in Ireland. At this date, she had yet to be transferred to the Isle of Man register. A rather more abstruse link with the letter i is that she worked occasionally as an irradiated fuel carrier at the time when the disposal of nuclear waste at sea was considered to be a practical proposition.

As the Russian vessel *Kapitan Vodenko* heads up the New Waterway towards Rotterdam, the *Jerome H* passes the Hook of Holland on 5 August 1994. She is heading for the Mediterranean and will make calls at Casablanca, Tunis and Marina di Carrara before returning to northern Europe and arriving at Glasgow on 8 September. Registered at Emden but flying the flag of Antigua and Barbuda, she was built in 1985 at the Hermann Surken shipyard in Papenburg, and she has kept her original name.

There can be little doubt that one of the most successful builders of coasters in post-war years has been the **J J** Sietas shipyard at Cranz, near Hamburg. The yard has been at the forefront of design and innovation, and has been responsive to changing economic circumstances and the demands of shipowners. The *Balmoral*, photographed in the Bristol Channel on 18 September 1986, is a classic example of early 1960s design. She began life in 1961 as the *Jacob Becker* and traded as such for the next thirteen years. In 1974, she was sold and moved to the Dutch flag, becoming the *Klazina*. In 1983, she was briefly renamed *Ina* and it was in 1984 that she became the *Balmoral*,

now flying the Maltese flag. In June 1987, she arrived at Harlingen and was laid up. By 1989, she had found a purchaser based in the eastern Mediterranean and she was renamed *Pirlant,* at first under the Turkish flag but then reverting to that of Malta. She settled into a trading pattern which mainly involved linking Famagusta to Izmir and Iskenderun. In January 1995, she was renamed *Zafer* and was once again under the Turkish flag. She has continued to trade on the same Mediterranean routes.

The **K**iel Canal celebrated its centenary in 1995, an event which was marked by much greater celebrations than those which marked the centenary of the Manchester Ship Canal a year earlier. The Kiel Canal links Holtenau, a suburb of Kiel, in the east to Brunsbuttel, on the lower Elbe, in the west. For ships passing between the North Sea and Baltic Sea, it offers a shorter and more sheltered passage than that via the Skaw on the northern tip of Denmark. For the coaster enthusiast, the Canal provides a wealth of interest with a constant stream of vessels passing the many vantage points on its banks. Heading eastwards on 13 August 1995 is the *Kormoran*. Owned by **K**laus Juls, she was built in 1965 at the Flensburg Shipyard in northern Germany and was named *Harle Riff* until 1972. In that year, she was renamed *Dorte Star* and then became *Millac Star* in 1981. She reverted to *Dorte Star* in 1984, keeping this name for five years before taking her current name in 1989. An attractive coaster, she is typical of many of her generation which now trade in Germany and the Baltic, an area for which her ice-strengthened hull makes her eminently suitable.

BM

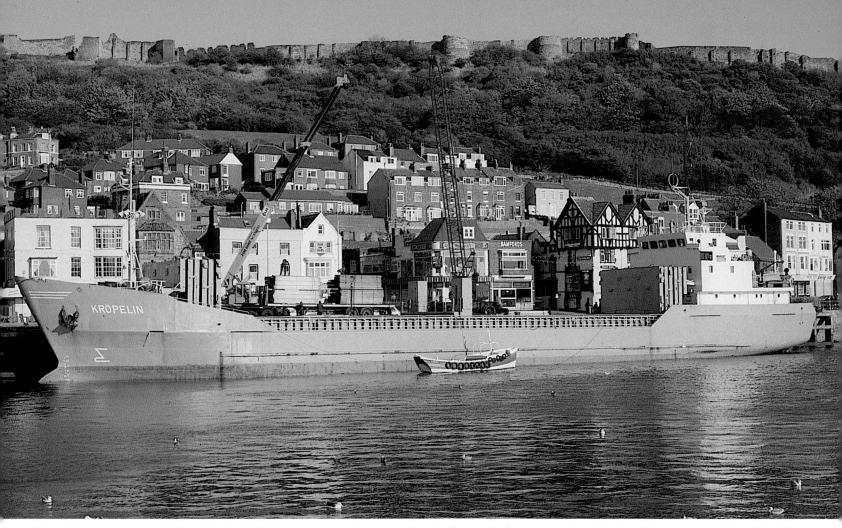

The German town of **K**ropelin is 25 kilometres south-west of Rostock, on the road towards Wismar and Lubeck in what was the former East Germany. Like many other towns in that country, it gave its name to a coaster. The vessel was one of a class of seven vessels built in the early 1970s at Boizenburg on the River Elbe. Two ships were delivered to the USSR and the remaining five went to the East German state shipping company, VEB Deutfracht of Rostock. Although built as container carriers with a container capacity of 62 TEU, they were often used in general cargo trades. The *Kropelin* is seen at Scarborough on 29 October 1986, discharging a cargo of timber. The port of

Scarborough has now virtually closed to commercial traffic. The early 1990s saw a trickle of vessels arrive but even this had dried up by mid-decade. The *Kropelin* has seen a definite change of role. Sold in 1992, she arrived at Bruges on 4 July 1992 and was laid up. She departed for Zaandam on 17 October of that year, flying the Cypriot flag and renamed *Star Aruba*. She was then converted into a tanker for use in the vegetable oil trade and became a regular visitor to Jurgens Jetty at Purfleet on the River Thames.

BM

In order to maximise earnings from a vessel, major surgery is sometimes undertaken. In the case of the *Shell Craftsman*, the surgery involved lengthening. The major oil companies have traditionally maintained a fleet of owned tankers for the distribution of products from refineries to depots, but the last decade has seen a decline in the use of owned tonnage and a greater reliance on the use of chartered ships. At the time of writing, BP, Esso and Shell each uses a handful of its own coastal tankers and the latter's *Shell Craftsman* is used as an illustration. Dating from 1968, she was Yard No. 937 from Hall Russell's Aberdeen shipyard. She was one of a series of ships built for Shell Mex/BP in the late 1960s (see the *BP Springer* on page 7) and, like all her near sisters, she was initially named after a refinery or depot belonging to Shell or BP. In her case, it was *Ardrossan*. In the late 1970s, there came an end to the joint marketing/distribution arrangement which linked Shell and BP, and the fleet was divided between the two constituent companies. The first change to affect the *Ardrossan* was the

repainting of her funnel into Shell colours - red with yellow scallop shell and black top. In 1979, the Shell tankers became more closely identified with the owning company by being given names prefixed with the word *Shell*, and the *Ardrossan* thus became *Shell Craftsman*. The next major changes came in 1991. On 8 March, she arrived at Sunderland to undergo a major life-extension refit which cost over £1 million. The addition of an extra 8.5 metre section increased her carrying capacity by some 500 cubic metres. Her electrical system was updated, and she was re-engined with a B & W Alpha diesel engine. Like other vessels in the fleet, she was now repainted from black to red and it is in this guise that she was photographed at Eastham when inward bound to load oil products at Stanlow on 13 August 1991. A further change in identity came in the summer of 1993 when she was renamed *Achatina*, thus continuing the Shell tradition of naming ships after shells and becoming the third holder of this name.

To have another lengthening may be considered a happy coincidence or possibly a deliberate ploy. Alternatively, the **L** could be for the **L**eer shipyard of Martin Janssen which constructed the *Jutta B* in 1965. More likely, though, our thoughts will centre on the **L** for **l**ocks for we see the gates closing in one of the lock chambers at Brunsbuttel on the Kiel Canal. It is a little after 7am on 21 July 1995 and the two ships have entered the lock from the River Elbe. The *Jutta B* began life as the *Gebina*, then becoming *Doris* in 1970. It was under this identity that she was lengthened in 1974. She was renamed *Hendrik* in 1978, and *Jutta B* in 1987. The coaster astern of the *Jutta B* is the *Pamela*, built by Hugo Peters at Wewelsfleth in 1985 and named *Boberg* until 1988.

The carriage of liquefied petroleum gas is inevitably hazardous and ships carrying such a cargo are often painted orange or red to maximise visibility. The *Happy Fellow*, photographed approaching Barry on 17 May 1988, has an interesting history. She was built as a conventional dry cargo vessel at Kristiansand in 1967 and was originally named *Teresa*. In 1970, she was renamed *Sunny Boy* and two years later was converted to a liquefied gas tanker by the addition of two carbon manganese steel tanks. In 1981, she changed from *Sunny Boy* to *Happy Fellow*. Rather than simply "growing up", the vessel had transferred from Norwegian ownership to Panamanian flag operators who were believed to be based in the Netherlands. For the next eleven years, she traded between the U.K. and continental ports. However, on 19 February 1992 she left Flushing for Abidjan, Ivory Coast, where she arrived on 11 March. Her next reported movement was from Abidjan to Las Palmas on 2 June. It was then reported that she was to be renamed *Kilgas Challenger* and under this name and the Bahamas flag, she was back at Abidjan on 21 October 1992. However, by mid-November she was in the River Tees and thus was back to her old, familiar haunts. By 1995, she was trading in Portugal usually between Lisbon and Sines but with occasional visits to Madeira. *BM*

The River Medway is one of the most important commercial waterways of southern England. Trading on its upper reaches has declined since the 1980s. Coasters still trade upriver as far as Snodland and there are plans to reactivate the wharf at Aylesford, on the outskirts of Maidstone. Most commercial traffic now uses port facilities at Sheerness and the Isle of Grain, and a little further upriver at Chatham. Many of the quaysides of the historic city of Rochester do still retain coastal traffic but its volume has declined considerably over the last few years. It was pleasing, therefore, to note the opening in 1995 of a new wharf at Frindsbury, near Strood, on the western bank of the river. This wharf is operated by Scot Line for the import of timber from Sweden. As is often the case, one port's gain is another's loss. In this instance, Scot Line left the Kent ports of Whitstable and Ridham Dock in favour of the River Medway. On 23 September 1995, the Valletta-registered *Berghav* had just arrived. This Norwegian-owned coaster has a history which is not typical of many of her compatriots. She was built in 1971 at the Bodewes yard in Hoogezand for German owner Hans Peterson, of Rendsburg. She traded as the *Christina* for this owner until 1985 when she was sold to Norway and renamed *Berghav*. Initially under the Norwegian flag, this has since changed for that of Malta.

The **M**anchester Ship Canal celebrated its centenary in 1994 and provides us with a letter **M**. Now but a shadow of its former self, it still sees a reasonable amount of traffic on its lower reaches notably between Runcorn and Eastham, where it joins the River Mersey. The decline of the manufacturing industries in central Lancashire has accounted for much of the traffic loss in the Canal's upper reaches, though the general transfer of freight from water to road transport is equally responsible. Also gone is the Lancashire coalfield, some of whose product used to be exported from Partington Coal Basin on the Canal. Regular callers loading coal for Ireland were the distinctive colliers owned by Belfast-based John Kelly Ltd. Outward bound for Ireland on 22 February 1980 is the *Ballylesson.* She dates from 1959 and was built by A Hall at Aberdeen. Lengthened in 1964, she left the Kelly fleet in 1982 and was renamed *Lino,* a name which she retained for a further five years before becoming the *Cristi* under the Honduran flag in 1987. This identity also lasted five years for she became *Samaa I* in 1992. She was noted in Dubai Creek in May of that year, seemingly laid up. A photograph of her taken at the time shows her with emerald green hull and white upperworks - very different from her distinctive yet drab Kelly colours. Her last recorded movement was from Aden to Ravenna in late December 1992. In 1994, it was reported that she had been renamed *G. Mother* under the Belize flag, but there have been no further movements reported.

BM

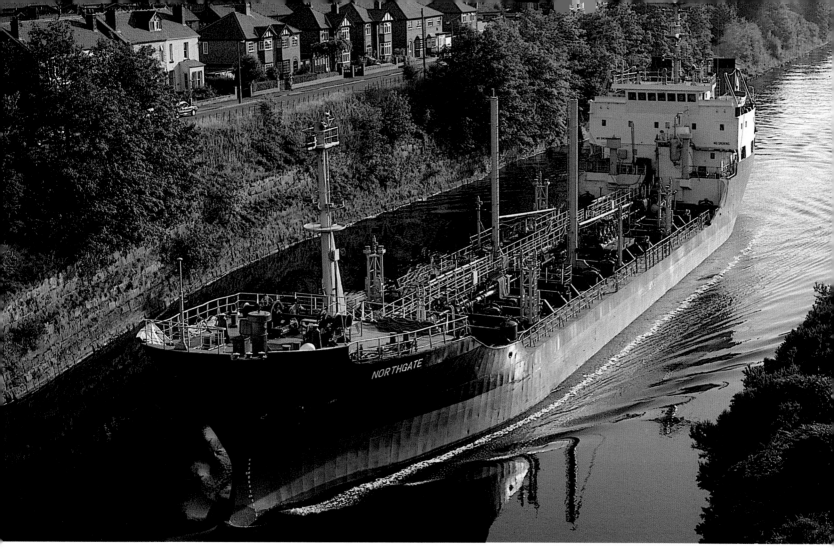

There are two bridges over the Manchester Ship Canal which offer excellent views of vessels passing beneath. The photograph on the previous page was taken from Warburton Bridge looking eastwards towards Manchester while this view is taken from Latchford High Level Bridge, Warrington, looking westwards towards Eastham. Heading up the Canal to Partington on 23 July 1990 is the *Northgate*, a tanker built in 1981 for the Hull Gates Shipping Company. Ownership was vested in Finance for Shipping Ltd and she was bareboat chartered to Hull Gates. On 4 October 1982, the share capital of Hull Gates was taken over by Rowbotham Tankships Ltd. which then took over the bareboat charter. The former Hull Gates tankers were incorporated into the Rowbotham fleet without a change of name, simply adopting the Rowbotham livery although not actually owned by Rowbotham. The *Northgate* is one of a group of four similar tankers built in Japan by Kanrei Zosen K K, Naruto. In 1990, P & O Bulk Shipping took a 50% stake in Rowbotham Tankships and took full control in 1993. Once again the *Northgate* found herself in new ownership and wearing new colours, this time the corporate blue of the P & O group.

BM

Normandy boasts much shipping activity, mainly centred on the major ports of Le Havre and Rouen. Honfleur, near the mouth of the River Seine, is certainly an attractive port but its importance is now mainly historical. It has a busy quay on the bank of the Seine but its inner docks see little activity. However, on 23 July 1985, the *Lisa Maria* was noted in port. She was built at the prolific Nordsovaerftet yard in Ringkobing. Looking very smart in this view, she had only just changed hands. What is particularly significant is that she had had a series of girls' names. Built as the *Ruth Lindinger*, she became *Ann Bach* in 1967, *Ann Charlott* in 1970, *Mette Viking* in 1975, *Birte Clipper* in 1978 - and, at the time of the photograph, *Lisa Maria*. She is one of those vessels which seems to change her identity at frequent intervals. She kept the name *Lisa Maria* for five years before becoming *Miranda* in 1990, though still in Danish ownership. At least she thus maintained the name theme. After leaving Colchester for Iceland on 17 February 1992, she was involved in a collision. She subsequently arrived at Fuglafjordur on 26 February and remained there until 24 March. She was then towed to the Danish port of Assens for permanent repairs. On 5 May, she sailed to Nyborg and at the end of that month, Lebanese owners took delivery and she departed for Beirut on 29 May, not arriving at that Lebanese port until 15 July. She was now named *Darin* under the Lebanese flag. This name was subsequently changed to *Darine*. In 1994, she transferred to Syrian ownership and became *Zena 2*.

BM

The *Nialed* was built at the Gebr. Coops shipyard at Hoogezand in 1960 as the *Saint Modan* for Glasgow shipowners and quarrymasters J & A Gardner. After serving them valiantly for almost 20 years, she was sold in 1979 and was renamed simply *Modan*. During the 1980s, she had a succession of owners and a succession of names, becoming *Nialed* in 1981, *Monica* (incorrectly listed as *Monique* in some sources) in 1982, *Nadir* in 1984 and *Sicom* in 1986. Under this name, she has been registered at Castries, St Lucia, and has traded in the West Indies, islands very different from those in Scotland and north-west England which she served when she began life as *Saint Modan*. She was photographed at the Parkkade, Rotterdam, on 31 May 1982.

BM

The concept of owner/captain has been an important one in coastal shipping until comparatively recently. However, the number of such owner/captains has declined considerably for a variety of reasons. There are still a handful working under the British flag, one of them being Guernsey-based Captain Derick Goubert. His *Mary Coast* is seen leaving Whitby on 5 August 1986. This attractive coaster was one of a series built for well-known Dutch coastal ship operator Wagenborg, of Delfzijl. She was the first of a group of four built at Appingedam and she was launched as the *Vechtborg* in 1961. Like several similar coasters, she moved on through a series of Netherlands-based owners, being renamed *Esperance* in 1972, *Noordster* in 1973, and *Finlandia* in 1975. She came into British ownership in November 1984 when purchased by Harris & Dixon Ltd., who renamed her *Mary Coast*

in April 1985. It was in November 1985 that Captain Goubert bought her. Perhaps the letter o could also be for orange, the colour of the vessel being very distinctive and known in the trade as "Goubert orange"! The *Mary Coast* remained in his ownership for five years before she found buyers in the Caribbean where she found gainful employment trading between Miami and Haiti and flying the Honduran flag. There is some confusion about the spelling of her name at this stage of her career. However, photographic evidence shows without doubt that the name on her bow was *Compassion de l'Eternel*. In 1991, it was reported that she was trading as the *Key Biscayne* under the Belize flag and then she was renamed *Splash* in 1993.

BM

There are two rivers in England named the **O**use which see coaster activity. This could arguably increase to three if the Great Ouse at King's Lynn is included. The focus of our attention in this photograph is not the Ouse which flows into the English Channel at Newhaven but rather the Ouse which joins the Humber and on which lie the ports of Goole, Selby and Howdendyke. It was from the latter that the *Resilience* had sailed on 22 July 1980. She was a purpose-built bulk starch carrier constructed for Crescent Shipping Ltd, of Rochester. Dating from 1969, her builders were the Voorwaarts shipyard at Martenshoek and she was specially designed for the delivery of starch from Delfzijl to Howdendyke and Otterham Quay. After the contract

had been won by a Dutch company, the *Resilience* was laid up at Otterham Quay on 27 April 1986. Reports that she would be converted to a cement carrier proved incorrect. In 1987 she was renamed *Kielder* following purchase by Effluents Services Ltd and was converted into an effluent tanker. She was usually to be found working in the north-east of England, often from an upriver base on the River Tees. In 1993, she was sold to Saudi Arabian owners and renamed *Al-Petrol Alzaher*, for use as a bunkering tanker at Jeddah - her third specialised use in her career.

BM

The approaches to many ports, both large and small, can be difficult and fraught with dangers to the navigator who is unaware of currents, channels, banks or tidal conditions. **P**ilots are, therefore, often mandatory or recommended. On 14 June 1994, the Berwick pilot boat goes alongside Crescent Shipping's *Crescence* to disembark the pilot who has assisted with navigation from Tweed Dock. This 1982-built coaster is one of a pair of coasters built by the defunct yard of Cubow Ltd, on the River Thames at Woolwich.

IW

P is for **p**recipitation! One dripping **p**hotographer plus one chink in a heavy cloud made for an intriguing shot of the *Fob 7* at Southampton on 16 April 1990. Standing on Berth 37, there would normally be a clear view along Southampton Water towards Fawley oil refinery but certainly not at this particular moment. The vessel is an interesting one and certainly not a conventional coaster. She was one of a series of what is believed to have been ten ships built in 1982 at the Santierul Naval yard in Galatz, Romania. They have been rarely mentioned in movement reports so it is difficult to trace their location and trade. The *Fob 8* was converted to a seismographic research ship in 1984, while the *Fob 9* and *Fob 10* were working along the west African coast in the 1980s, the former seemingly based at Pointe Noire. Both of these vessels were back at Galatz in 1990. Reverting to the *Fob 7*, in 1990 she was chartered from her Norwegian owners by Solent Seatruck Ltd. It was the intention to operate a daily lift-on/lift-off service from Southampton to the Isle of Wight, mainly for dangerous cargoes which would otherwise use the passenger ferries. Although she did make several trips, and even visited Jersey, the service was not successful and she was returned to her owner in October 1990.

The summer of 1985 was a bad one for small, water-served oil distribution depots for it saw the closure of many of them - see page 17. The BP depot at Quedgeley on the outskirts of Gloucester was a further victim of this spate of closures and a consequence of this was a catastrophic decline in the volume of shipping using the Sharpness - Gloucester canal. In the late 1960s, tanker owners Bowker and King ordered half a dozen vessels of the maximum size for safe navigation of this Canal, and these vessels served Quedgeley on an almost daily basis from Swansea. The *Bisley*, photographed at Quedgeley on 2 May 1983, was built at Richard Dunston's Hessle yard in 1969, and remained in the Bowker & King fleet (which was subsumed with Crescent Shipping into the Hays Group) until sold to Greek owners in late 1990 when she became the *Naoussa*.

BM

The *Quality Spirit* began life as the *Bastiaan Broere*, built in 1968 at the Nieuwe Noord Nederlandse Shipyard, Groningen, for Gebr. Broere, of Dordrecht. Her 14 tanks enabled her to carry a wide range of oil and chemical cargoes. She spent twenty years in the Broere fleet before being sold to Cypriot-flag operators in 1988, along with her near sister (?brother) *Jacobus Broere* which became *Quality Trader*. Both ships continued to trade in a pattern similar to that which preceded their sale and it was not unusual to find them in the New Waterway where the *Quality Spirit* was photographed on 30 May 1991. Later in 1991, this vessel was sold and renamed *George V* under the Panamanian flag. She now found work in the Mediterranean, frequently calling at Italian ports such as Formia and Genoa. By early 1993, she had been renamed *Francis* and was transferred to the Maltese flag. However, in 1995 her owners were noted as a Palermo-based company and she was flying the Italian flag. It was something of a surprise when she was observed at Europoort in August 1995.

BM

The port of **R**otterdam has many claims to fame, far more than could possibly be included in a book such as this. The ship enthusiast can never be sure what will be found at the quaysides, especially in the older dock areas. Always a source of interest are the coasters lying at the Parkkade, possibly awaiting their next orders, maybe repairing, or perhaps laid up or in the process of sale. On 30 May 1985, the *Safir* had recently been renamed. She was built in 1965 at the Oskarshamn shipyard as the *Bore IV* and with her Ice Class 1 certificate was ideally suited for the export trade of forest products and paper from her native Finland. Her first change of identity came in 1972 when she was renamed *Kare*. She spent the next ten years on the Goole - Finland Line service, linking Finnish ports such as Helsinki and Turku to the east coast of England. On 14 August 1982, she arrived at Turku

and was laid up there for over a year. Back in service in 1984, she was available for sale and found Maltese-flag buyers in the spring of 1985. Although it was at first thought that she would trade in the Mediterranean, this was not the case. On 26 January 1986, she left Hamburg on a voyage to Canada. The voyage had its problems and it was not until 28 April that she arrived in Montreal. Early in the following year, she was reported sold and was towed from the Canadian port of Sept Iles in mid-January. Her new owners were noted as Scan Star Ltd, of Helsinki, although she remained under the Maltese flag and was now trading as the *Jennastar*. Her end came on 21 December 1988 when she sank while on passage from Sousse to Spain. All her crew were rescued.

BM

The Isle of Man-based **R**amsey Steamship Company was established in 1913 by a group of seven local businessmen. Since then it has served the island (or the mainland, according to those who live on the Isle of Man!) for over 80 years, often in the shadow of the Isle of Man Steam Packet Company because of the latter's connection with the passenger trade. The Ramsey Steamship fleet has never been large, nor have the vessels in it been large. All its ships have had names prefixed by the word "Ben" which is the Manx word for "woman". Built at Wroclaw, Poland in 1977, the *Ben Vane* was one of a group of six vessels. She traded under the British flag as the *Julia S* until 1981 when she hoisted the Cyprus flag after being sold and renamed *Bulk Moon*. She was purchased by Ramsey Steamship in 1988. In this view, she is seen at Glasson Dock on 13 April 1994, loading coal for her home port of Ramsey. It is the transport of coal, and other bulk products, across the Irish Sea that has been the company's staple work over the years.

River/sea vessels are now regularly seen in many ports. The idea of a ship having the capability of trading along canals and to upriver destinations has many attractions. On the Thames, the "flat-irons" (or flatties) used to be a familiar sight easing their way under the bridges as they made their way to and from the upriver power stations and gas works. From the late 1970s, western European shipbuilders developed the concept and new designs of seagoing ships began to call at inland locations such as Basle, Lyon and Vienna. **R**ussia, meanwhile, had also been building vessels which could sail along the vast domestic river/canal systems and also trade on open seas. Following the collapse of the former Soviet Union, the number of these river/sea ships engaged in international trade has grown considerably and classes of ships previously confined to inland work are now being adapted for more general trade. At the time of writing, some eighteen classes of "Russian" river/sea ships have been identified, several of which are divided into two or more sub-classes. Voyages from the U. K. to the Caspian Sea via the heart of Russia are not unusual. To illustrate the type, we look at an example of the newer breed of Russian river/sea ship. She is the *Sormovskiy 3063*, built in 1989 at Viana do Castelo in Portugal. On 21 July 1991, she arrived at Creetown, in Wigtown Bay on the northern shore of the Solway Firth, to load high quality armour rock granite for delivery to Kent where the rock would be used in new sea defences at Herne Bay. It had been a decade since Creetown had seen a ship, and she was far bigger than any other vessel to use the jetty. Indeed, local opinion was that she was simply too big. This was certainly not so. Our photograph shows her on a later visit heading back into Wigtown Bay on 21 August 1991 after she was unable to berth because the tide had failed to reach the predicted height and consequently a loaded vessel at the jetty was unable to leave.

One of the foremost operators of river/sea ships is **S**eacon Limited, whose UK operation is based on the River Thames at Millwall. Here is situated the only purpose-built steel transit terminal in the U.K. and it is furthermore the most inland berth on the River Thames to receive seagoing ships on a regular basis. Seacon is a firm believer in the concept of waterborne delivery of goods to the furthest point possible, and its vessels are seen in locations such as Basle and the centre of Paris. It is not surprising, therefore, that all its coasters are low air draught vessels capable of such inland navigation. All are chartered and, once within the company's operation, are renamed using the prefix "Sea" followed usually by the name of a European river. The *Sea Ems* was built in 1984 at the Julius Diedrich shipyard, at Oldersum near Emden, thus establishing a strong link with the river from which she takes her name. She was photographed in a rare shaft of sunlight on the gloomy evening of 19 June 1992, as she headed up the River Humber.

BM

A theme shared by this and the following page is that of shipbuilding, but what contrasts are found. We begin at the Selby yard of Cochrane Shipbuilders Ltd, and find the *Boston Sea Lance* fitting out on 15 July 1979, just three days after her launch. A refrigerated cargo ship, she was being built for the Boston Deep Sea Fisheries group and certainly made a change from the trawlers which comprised the rest of her owner's fleet. In 1983, she was sold to Dutch associates of the North British Maritime Group and renamed *Norbrit Vries.* Built as a 3-hatch/3-hold vessel, her new operators felt that this was insufficient and so in 1985 they lengthened her by adding an additional hold and two further hatches. By 1988, she was operating under the flag of the Bahamas and in this year she was renamed *Fenland* after ownership was transferred to the Seatrade Groningen group.

BM

We make no apology for portraying yet another coaster from the shipyard of J J Sietas, though we can claim extra points here for the Stade-registered *Condor* is on her way up the River Seine to St Etienne du Rouvray, a few kilometres up river from Rouen, with a cargo of china clay slurry from Cornwall on 31 May 1990.

Built in 1978, she was the first in a class known as Type 104 and she was the first in what would be a group of five coasters equipped with two 125-tonne capacity stainless steel tanks, one fore and one aft, for the carriage of china clay in slurry form.

We now look at yet another Sietas vessel although she is used to illustrate the letter **T**. The *Arklow River* is a purpose-built cement carrier. She was launched at the Sietas yard on 5 February 1972, bearing the name *Milburn Carrier* and destined to work for New Zealand Cement Holdings Ltd. She spent most of her time trading in the Napier/Westport area. She was purchased by Arklow Shipping in 1989 and left Lyttleton for Dublin on 6 April 1989, bearing her new name and Arklow registry but in her old colours. She passed through the Panama Canal on 15 May and eventually arrived in Dublin on 4 June. She eventually entered service for her new owners on 24 June and initially delivered cement from Drogheda to Newport and Sharpness. Since then she has traded more widely and, indeed, in the summer of 1995 she was working between Setubal and Madeira. Our photograph, dated 9 October 1995, shows her off the Blue Circle Cement Works, Northfleet, and she thus illustrates the River **T**hames.

IW

From the mighty River **T**hames, we move to the magnificent River **T**weed. Renowned for its beauty, its fishing and the majestic Royal Border Bridge at Berwick, it sees a considerable quantity of coastal traffic as noted on page 7. This colourful view captures the *Sival* in the river estuary on 3 April 1993. She had arrived to load a cargo of 718 tonnes of cement for delivery to Kirkwall. She began life in 1961 as the *Reinhard Danz*, built at the Husum shipyard for Hamburg owner Karl Heinrich Danz. She was purchased by Danish owners in 1969 and was renamed *Stevnsboen*, moving on in 1977 to her owner at the time of the photograph, following the loss of a previous vessel named *Sival*.

In 1993, she moved on to Liberian-flag owners and her name was topped and tailed to *Iva*. She was seen briefly under this name at European ports in the spring of 1993. However, on 29 May, she left Dordrecht for her intended new sphere of trade. After calling at Setubal in early June, she crossed the Atlantic and arrived at Demerara on 25 June and then Cristobal on 14 July. In 1994, she was sold on yet again, now becoming *Chubasco II*, under the Honduran flag. She now trades between Colombia and Panama, calling at ports such as Barranquilla, Mamonal and Coco Solo.

Not T for Teignmouth but **U** for **U**nion Transport, a leading name in European coastal shipping. Using a slightly different viewpoint from that found on the cover of this book, we see the *Union Venus* leaving Teignmouth on 13 April 1987. She was one of four sisterships built for Union Transport in 1981 by the prolific yard of Nordsovaerftet, in the Danish port of Ringkobing. Under the Irish flag, she remained with Union Transport until early 1984 when she was sold, transferred to the Cypriot flag and renamed *Waterway*. Union Transport was established in 1946 as shipbrokers and forwarding agents, though it was not until 1973 that it began to own ships.

BM

Double stamps (or is it quad?) for **Uu**sikaupunki! This small port is to be found on the western coast of Finland. It is a flourishing town whose maritime centre is now a marina although there is varied commercial shipping activity away from the centre. This includes a roll on/roll off ferry service to Sweden and a berth for small tankers. However, most of the commercial vessels call at the private wharf which serves the Kemira fertiliser factory and it is at this wharf that the German *Selene Prahm* was photographed on 24 July 1995. She was discharging a cargo of 2,200 tonnes of magnesium sulphate loaded in Bremen. The vessel is a product of the Koetter Shipyard in Haren/Ems and was built in 1994 for owners Hammann and Prahm. Although well suited to the carriage of bulk cargoes, she is generally to be found conveying timber from Sweden and Finland to the United Kingdom. Indeed, after leaving Uusikaupunki, she made the short voyage north to Mantyluoto where she loaded a cargo of timber for delivery to Hull.

BM

The Groningen-based shipping company Beck's is well known in coastal shipping circles not only in the Netherlands but throughout Europe. Over the years, succeeding generations of ships have steadily increased in size but they always remain smartly turned out with their grey hulls and blue funnels. Awaiting her turn to load china clay at Fowey on 27 March 1989 was the *Ventura*. She was built at the Bodewes Gruno yard, Foxhol, in 1972. After a career of 22 years in the Beck fleet, she was purchased by other Dutch owners, Gebr. Bruins, in 1994 and was renamed *Hendrik B* under the flag of St Vincent and Grenadines. On 29 December 1994, she suffered heavy weather damage while on passage from Uddevalla to Reykjavik. Temporary repairs were effected at the latter port following her arrival there on New Year's Day, 1995, and following further temporary repairs at Delfzijl, she arrived at Rotterdam in early February. There she was purchased by associates of Rochester-based Thomas Watson (Shipping) Ltd, and she moved to Hull on 9 March 1995 for permanent repairs. She currently trades in the Watson-operated fleet as *Lady Sandra*.

BM

The port of **V**ejle is situated on the east coast of Jylland (Jutland) in Denmark. On a typical day, it will have half a dozen coasters lining its quays. On 1 August 1992, we find the Danish coaster *Thuro* discharging limestone from Fakse Ladeplads on the south-west coast of Sjaelland (Zeeland). She spends much time in this trade, loading regularly at Fakse Ladeplads and delivering her cargoes to ports such as Grenaa and Odense in addition to Vejle. She was built as the *Stevnsklint* in 1963 at the Husumer Shipyard, and was renamed *Uno* in 1981. In May 1991, she was involved in a "name exchange" with another coaster, an event guaranteed to cause confusion and consternation among ship enthusiasts. A 1954-built *Thuro* had been trading between Fakse Ladeplads and Vejle. She became *Uno* while docked at Soby in late May 1991. The 1963-built *Uno* had arrived at Soby earlier in the month and it was here that the double name change was effected. *BM*

57

The Hull-based shipowner John H **W**hitaker (Tankers) Ltd has expanded into ownership of larger vessels during the 1990s. The company has long been associated with barges and estuarial craft but it has now purchased various second-hand coastal tankers in order to offer a wider range of bunkering services and oil/petroleum products transport. The *Whithaven* has had a varied career. She was built in 1972 by Appledore Shipbuilders as the *Caernarvon* for the Shell Mex Group. When this fleet was divided between the constituent BP and Shell companies in the late 1970s, she joined the Shell ships and was renamed *Shell Director* in 1979. In 1993, she was sold to the Gravesend-based tanker owners C Crawley Ltd and was renamed *Frank C.* This company resembles the Whitaker company in many ways, though it is somewhat smaller. Thanks to the steady expansion of bunkering work in the Bristol Channel, Whitakers considered the *Frank C* an ideal ship for this work and she was purchased and renamed *Whithaven* in 1993. We see her here on 2 June 1995 as she hurries up the Bristol Channel towards Avonmouth taking 170 tons of fuel oil and 25 tons of gas oil to the Bell Lines container ship *Jana*. BM

The light blue hull colour of coasters operated by Bergen-based Paal Wilson is a familiar sight in many European ports, especially on the east coast of the United Kingdom. Wilson ships also maintain important links between Norway and the lower Rhine ports and Rotterdam. Characteristic of the fleet is the *Hedlo*, a 1971 product of the Orens yard at Trondheim. She has remained in the fleet under her original name, although she currently flies the flag of the Bahamas. She was lengthened in 1979 and the effect of this modification can be clearly seen in this overhead view of her off the Hook of Holland on 5 August 1988.

BM

X is for.....?? We may have a problem here so I hope that readers will allow Exmouth! There were few in the shipping world who did not lament the closure of this attractive and successful small Devon port at the end of 1989. Plans for its "redevelopment" have proceeded but slowly and it would appear to prove that it is working ports which generate prosperity for a community as they support a wide variety of ancilliary trades and industries. The *Marant,* photographed on 19 May 1982, was discharging 490 tonnes of soya meal. She was built at Appingedam in 1967 as the *Gretina Holwerda.* She kept this name until 1981 when she became *Marant.* There must have been some good fortune in observing her under this name for later in the year she was renamed *Deo Volente.* She had remained under the Dutch flag from her launch and she spent a further ten years under this flag until she arrived at Harlingen on 4 May 1992. She was then handed over to Honduras-flag operators and renamed *Nathalia.* After brief visits to Goole, Rotterdam and Antwerp, she crossed the Atlantic to work for her new owners in the Colombia/Panama area. Like the former *Sival* (see page 53), she visits Coco Solo and Barranquilla but also visits Aruba. *BM*

Photographed at Eastham on 26 July 1989, the *Yuma* is a multi-purpose tanker, built to carry molasses in addition to mineral and vegetable oils. She is a 1969 product of the Lindenau shipyard at Kiel which built her for German owners Atlantic-Rhederei F & W Joch. Like all vessels in this owner's fleet, she was named after an American Indian tribe, the Yuma being natives of the southern United States and Mexico. In 1991, she was sold to Garnet Shipping, of Malta, but she remained under the German flag as *Johanna*. Initially, she continued to trade in northern Europe but by the summer of 1991, she had changed to the flag of Malta and was based in the Mediterranean. Despite this, a molasses cargo would occasionally bring her back north and she delivered such a cargo to Bristol's Royal Portbury Dock on 16 January 1992. She even came very near to the location of this photograph twice in late 1994 when she delivered two cargoes from Brest to Liverpool. By the summer of 1995, she was trading under the St Vincent and Grenadines flag and working out of Durban. So, for a tanker of modest size, she has traded widely during the last five years.

BM

The story of British shipbuilding since the 1970s has been one of almost unrelieved gloom as yard after yard has closed, engineering and manufacturing skills have been lost, and communities have been compelled to seek other kinds of labour in order to survive. One of the few shipbuilding companies to maintain its standing through these difficult years has been the Yorkshire Drydock Company, based in Hull and a subsidiary of the Whitaker group of companies. In the mid-1970s, it built estuarial barges for use on the River Mersey and Manchester Ship Canal, and then used this design to develop what has become known as the "Yorkshire Coaster", a standard class of vessel capable of trading economically to upriver ports. The series began with the delivery in 1982 of the *Hoo Venture* to the Medway-based owners R Lapthorn & Co Ltd. She was followed by the *Hoocreek*, photographed leaving Teignmouth on 10 April 1995.

BM

The *Zealence* was built in 1979 at the now-defunct yard of J W Cook, at Wivenhoe. She began life working for Spillers as the *Birkenhead Miller* and was the second of a pair of near sisterships which have followed identical careers. In 1982, she entered the fleet of Crescent Shipping and was renamed *Zealence* while her sister, the *London Miller*, became *Yulence*. After five years in Crescent ownership, both vessels moved on to an associate company of Cardiff-based Charles M Willie & Co Ltd. Our vessel became the *Iberian Ocean* while the *Yulence* became the *Iberian Coast*, both registered in Nassau and therefore flying the Bahamas flag. The *Zealence* is seen on 18 April 1987 at Dunball Wharf, on the River Parrett near Bridgwater. In the early 1990s, this wharf saw a steady decline in trade. Like many other such wharves, it suffered from the abolition of the National Dock Labour Scheme. It looked as though Dunball was destined for closure. However, in the late summer of 1995, the wharf was purchased by a local haulage company with the hope of a big increase in throughput. *BM*

Just as we began with a letter of the Greek alphabet, so we end with one. In fact the final letter of the Greek alphabet is "omega" but it suits the purposes of this volume to end with zeta. This is the name of the vessel photographed in Piraeus roads on 8 August 1984. A chemical tanker, she was built as the *Lucy Essberger* at the J G Hitzler yard, Lauenburg, in 1967. She remained in the Essberger fleet until 1983 when she was sold to the Zeta Maritime Company, of Piraeus, and renamed *Zeta*. She was renamed in 1989 and by an eminently suitable coincidence, at least for our purposes, her new name was *Fair Alpha*.

BM